# Questions lovingly answered by:

_____________  &  _____________

How do I love thee? Let me count the ways.
I love thee to the depth and breadth and height
My soul can reach, when feeling out of sight
For the ends of being and ideal grace.
I love thee to the level of every day's
Most quiet need, by sun and candle-light.
I love thee freely, as men strive for right.
I love thee purely, as they turn from praise.
I love thee with the passion put to use
In my old griefs, and with my childhood's faith.
I love thee with a love I seemed to lose
With my lost saints. I love thee with the breath,
Smiles, tears, of all my life; and, if God choose,
I shall but love thee better after death.

— Elizabeth Barrett Browning —

## What is an exciting or crazy trip you have taken?

☐ HER REPLY  ☐ HIS REPLY                 ☐ HIS REPLY  ☐ HER REPLY

## What do you think the future of fiction will be?

☐ HER REPLY  ☐ HIS REPLY                 ☐ HIS REPLY  ☐ HER REPLY

# List of things that might benefit the system

☐ HER REPLY ☐ HIS REPLY

☐ HIS REPLY ☐ HER REPLY

# Why are we speaking in the third person?

☐ HER REPLY ☐ HIS REPLY

☐ HIS REPLY ☐ HER REPLY

# What would you change about yourself?

☐ HER REPLY ☐ HIS REPLY

☐ HIS REPLY ☐ HER REPLY

# What human trait is useful now but would have been disadvantageous in the past?

☐ HER REPLY ☐ HIS REPLY

☐ HIS REPLY ☐ HER REPLY

# Why do you think your hair is so fine?

☐ HER REPLY  ☐ HIS REPLY

☐ HIS REPLY  ☐ HER REPLY

# Would you rather have a giant robot or a sloth?

☐ HER REPLY  ☐ HIS REPLY

☐ HIS REPLY  ☐ HER REPLY

# What does your biggest dream look like?

☐ HER REPLY ☐ HIS REPLY

☐ HIS REPLY ☐ HER REPLY

# If there was one person who you had the power of giving immortality to, who would it be and why?

☐ HER REPLY ☐ HIS REPLY

☐ HIS REPLY ☐ HER REPLY

# What is the most significant thing you have learned today?

☐ HER REPLY  ☐ HIS REPLY

☐ HIS REPLY  ☐ HER REPLY

# If you had to choose one thing on the list that you wanted to see the most improved this year, which would that be?

☐ HER REPLY  ☐ HIS REPLY

☐ HIS REPLY  ☐ HER REPLY

# If you could be anyone for one hour and it would change your life, who would it be?

☐ HER REPLY ☐ HIS REPLY

☐ HIS REPLY ☐ HER REPLY

# What kind of love do you have?

☐ HER REPLY ☐ HIS REPLY

☐ HIS REPLY ☐ HER REPLY

# If you had to choose one thing you wanted, what would it be and why?

☐ HER REPLY  ☐ HIS REPLY                    ☐ HIS REPLY  ☐ HER REPLY

# Do you like doing sports? Why?

☐ HER REPLY  ☐ HIS REPLY                    ☐ HIS REPLY  ☐ HER REPLY

# How do you know what is real and what isn't?

☐ HER REPLY ☐ HIS REPLY

☐ HIS REPLY ☐ HER REPLY

# What something about your work that you can take pride in?

☐ HER REPLY ☐ HIS REPLY

☐ HIS REPLY ☐ HER REPLY

☐ HER REPLY   ☐ HIS REPLY                    ☐ HIS REPLY   ☐ HER REPLY

If you had to choose one thing from your childhood that you would want back, what would it be?

☐ HER REPLY   ☐ HIS REPLY                    ☐ HIS REPLY   ☐ HER REPLY

# Do you have anything you feel was missing from your past life?

☐ HER REPLY  ☐ HIS REPLY        ☐ HIS REPLY  ☐ HER REPLY

# What is one thing that you are passionate about and why?

☐ HER REPLY  ☐ HIS REPLY        ☐ HIS REPLY  ☐ HER REPLY

If you had to choose one thing to get back into shape, what would it be?

☐ HER REPLY ☐ HIS REPLY

☐ HIS REPLY ☐ HER REPLY

Did you enjoy your early career? Why?

☐ HER REPLY ☐ HIS REPLY

☐ HIS REPLY ☐ HER REPLY

If you had to choose one thing from a list of things you wish you could get to know more about, what would it be?

☐ HER REPLY   ☐ HIS REPLY

☐ HIS REPLY   ☐ HER REPLY

What qualities and acts do you have that make you the best character in the world?

☐ HER REPLY   ☐ HIS REPLY

☐ HIS REPLY   ☐ HER REPLY

# What makes it so different?

☐ HER REPLY  ☐ HIS REPLY

☐ HIS REPLY  ☐ HER REPLY

# List of things that you can do for lack of skill

☐ HER REPLY  ☐ HIS REPLY

☐ HIS REPLY  ☐ HER REPLY

## What are you doing when you're not talking to someone?

☐ HER REPLY  ☐ HIS REPLY

☐ HIS REPLY  ☐ HER REPLY

## What can you say to a stranger in an elevator to make that stranger feel at ease?

☐ HER REPLY  ☐ HIS REPLY

☐ HIS REPLY  ☐ HER REPLY

# What is something that no one has ever told you before?

□ HER REPLY  □ HIS REPLY

□ HIS REPLY  □ HER REPLY

# What is your favorite dish around the world?

□ HER REPLY  □ HIS REPLY

□ HIS REPLY  □ HER REPLY

# Do you have high aspirations or low ones? Why?

☐ HER REPLY ☐ HIS REPLY　　　　☐ HIS REPLY ☐ HER REPLY

# If you had to choose one thing about yourself that you would change if you could, what would it be?

☐ HER REPLY ☐ HIS REPLY　　　　☐ HIS REPLY ☐ HER REPLY

# What were some of the major things that made you who you are?

☐ HER REPLY  ☐ HIS REPLY

☐ HIS REPLY  ☐ HER REPLY

# What is the one thing you'd change about the past 20 years?

☐ HER REPLY  ☐ HIS REPLY

☐ HIS REPLY  ☐ HER REPLY

# What's your favorite kind of chocolate?

☐ HER REPLY   ☐ HIS REPLY                    ☐ HIS REPLY   ☐ HER REPLY

# How do you deal with people who think as you think?

☐ HER REPLY   ☐ HIS REPLY                    ☐ HIS REPLY   ☐ HER REPLY

# List of things that stood in the way

☐ HER REPLY   ☐ HIS REPLY                ☐ HIS REPLY   ☐ HER REPLY

# Where did your mind go?

☐ HER REPLY   ☐ HIS REPLY                ☐ HIS REPLY   ☐ HER REPLY

## Are you just always willing to push through? Why?

☐ HER REPLY ☐ HIS REPLY

_______________________________
_______________________________
_______________________________
_______________________________
_______________________________
_______________________________
_______________________________
_______________________________

☐ HIS REPLY ☐ HER REPLY

_______________________________
_______________________________
_______________________________
_______________________________
_______________________________
_______________________________
_______________________________
_______________________________

## What are the top five things you think of as being in your life?

☐ HER REPLY ☐ HIS REPLY

_______________________________
_______________________________
_______________________________
_______________________________
_______________________________
_______________________________
_______________________________
_______________________________

☐ HIS REPLY ☐ HER REPLY

_______________________________
_______________________________
_______________________________
_______________________________
_______________________________
_______________________________
_______________________________
_______________________________

*What's your favorite book that you've read in the past year?*

☐ HER REPLY  ☐ HIS REPLY

☐ HIS REPLY  ☐ HER REPLY

*Say something that will make them uncomfortable but doesn't make them angry or offended.*

☐ HER REPLY  ☐ HIS REPLY

☐ HIS REPLY  ☐ HER REPLY

# What were the other things you tried to do that didn't work?

☐ HER REPLY  ☐ HIS REPLY                    ☐ HIS REPLY  ☐ HER REPLY

# When was the last time you made an investment that gave you a sense of hope?

☐ HER REPLY  ☐ HIS REPLY                    ☐ HIS REPLY  ☐ HER REPLY

# List of things that you've seen that are not supposed to be there

☐ HER REPLY ☐ HIS REPLY

☐ HIS REPLY ☐ HER REPLY

# Why do you keep on complaining about the weather?

☐ HER REPLY ☐ HIS REPLY

☐ HIS REPLY ☐ HER REPLY

# When was the last time you laughed out loud in front of someone?

☐ HER REPLY ☐ HIS REPLY

☐ HIS REPLY ☐ HER REPLY

# What does your son look for in a friend?

☐ HER REPLY ☐ HIS REPLY

☐ HIS REPLY ☐ HER REPLY

# How do you feel about criticism?

☐ HER REPLY  ☐ HIS REPLY

☐ HIS REPLY  ☐ HER REPLY

# How do you deal with pride?

☐ HER REPLY  ☐ HIS REPLY

☐ HIS REPLY  ☐ HER REPLY

# Will you be happy tomorrow? Why?

☐ HER REPLY  ☐ HIS REPLY

☐ HIS REPLY  ☐ HER REPLY

# Would you rather have that man or a dog in your home?

☐ HER REPLY  ☐ HIS REPLY

☐ HIS REPLY  ☐ HER REPLY

What would you consider the top 3 services in your life today?

☐ HER REPLY  ☐ HIS REPLY                    ☐ HIS REPLY  ☐ HER REPLY

What is most important to you to be able to reveal your feelings about people and to be able to handle relationships?

☐ HER REPLY  ☐ HIS REPLY                    ☐ HIS REPLY  ☐ HER REPLY

# What makes you think we would look at that situation differently?

☐ HER REPLY ☐ HIS REPLY

☐ HIS REPLY ☐ HER REPLY

# What possession do you cherish the most?

☐ HER REPLY ☐ HIS REPLY

☐ HIS REPLY ☐ HER REPLY

# Say something about your true feelings

☐ HER REPLY  ☐ HIS REPLY

☐ HIS REPLY  ☐ HER REPLY

# Which is more important to you, to be fed with the real truth or to receive fake information?

☐ HER REPLY  ☐ HIS REPLY

☐ HIS REPLY  ☐ HER REPLY

# Would you rather do a thing or a million things together or separately?

☐ HER REPLY  ☐ HIS REPLY

__________________________
__________________________
__________________________
__________________________
__________________________
__________________________
__________________________
__________________________
__________________________

☐ HIS REPLY  ☐ HER REPLY

__________________________
__________________________
__________________________
__________________________
__________________________
__________________________
__________________________
__________________________
__________________________

# What is most important to you to do?

☐ HER REPLY  ☐ HIS REPLY

__________________________
__________________________
__________________________
__________________________
__________________________
__________________________

☐ HIS REPLY  ☐ HER REPLY

__________________________
__________________________
__________________________
__________________________
__________________________
__________________________

# What is the one thing you dislike more than anything else?

☐ HER REPLY  ☐ HIS REPLY    ☐ HIS REPLY  ☐ HER REPLY

# Would you rather sit in a room with ten scientists from the International Space Station or four astronauts from the Curiosity Mars rover?

☐ HER REPLY  ☐ HIS REPLY    ☐ HIS REPLY  ☐ HER REPLY

## When do you want to spend your money?

☐ HER REPLY  ☐ HIS REPLY          ☐ HIS REPLY  ☐ HER REPLY

## What is a great gift?

☐ HER REPLY  ☐ HIS REPLY          ☐ HIS REPLY  ☐ HER REPLY

# What's your most inspiring moment?

☐ HER REPLY  ☐ HIS REPLY

☐ HIS REPLY  ☐ HER REPLY

# Which is more important to you, to prepare for the future or to enjoy the present?

☐ HER REPLY  ☐ HIS REPLY

☐ HIS REPLY  ☐ HER REPLY

# Who should your enemies be and why?

☐ HER REPLY ☐ HIS REPLY

☐ HIS REPLY ☐ HER REPLY

# What is one thing you have in common with the people that supported you in the past?

☐ HER REPLY ☐ HIS REPLY

☐ HIS REPLY ☐ HER REPLY

# What is the longest time you've lived alone?

☐ HER REPLY  ☐ HIS REPLY

☐ HIS REPLY  ☐ HER REPLY

# What do you feel the worst thing about?

☐ HER REPLY  ☐ HIS REPLY

☐ HIS REPLY  ☐ HER REPLY

# What causes you to be more likely to be successful?

☐ HER REPLY ☐ HIS REPLY

☐ HIS REPLY ☐ HER REPLY

# What is the most important thing for you right now?

☐ HER REPLY ☐ HIS REPLY

☐ HIS REPLY ☐ HER REPLY

# What's the worst advice you've ever gotten?

☐ HER REPLY  ☐ HIS REPLY

☐ HIS REPLY  ☐ HER REPLY

# Say something about the way you're looking at things.

☐ HER REPLY  ☐ HIS REPLY

☐ HIS REPLY  ☐ HER REPLY

# What was you happiest when you were little?

☐ HER REPLY  ☐ HIS REPLY

☐ HIS REPLY  ☐ HER REPLY

# Would you rather work with someone who gets paid to make games or one you'd rather learn from and get paid to make games?

☐ HER REPLY  ☐ HIS REPLY

☐ HIS REPLY  ☐ HER REPLY

If you had to live in one place for the rest of your life, where would you choose and why?

☐ HER REPLY   ☐ HIS REPLY                    ☐ HIS REPLY   ☐ HER REPLY

If you could bring your mother from another world to the Earth, what would you name her?

☐ HER REPLY   ☐ HIS REPLY                    ☐ HIS REPLY   ☐ HER REPLY

# What is the source of the person's worst ideas?

☐ HER REPLY  ☐ HIS REPLY

☐ HIS REPLY  ☐ HER REPLY

# Have you ever been cheated on?

☐ HER REPLY  ☐ HIS REPLY

☐ HIS REPLY  ☐ HER REPLY

# What are you looking forward to?





# List of things that I do to make other people happy

# Write about a dream you can remember.

☐ HER REPLY  ☐ HIS REPLY

☐ HIS REPLY  ☐ HER REPLY

# Imagine trading places with the first person you spoke to today. What would you feel?

☐ HER REPLY  ☐ HIS REPLY

☐ HIS REPLY  ☐ HER REPLY

# In what way do you think your experience has had some benefits?

☐ HER REPLY  ☐ HIS REPLY                    ☐ HIS REPLY  ☐ HER REPLY

# If you had to choose one thing to give up for your life, what would it be?

☐ HER REPLY  ☐ HIS REPLY                    ☐ HIS REPLY  ☐ HER REPLY

# Do you feel like people still have a sense of kindness these days? Why?

☐ HER REPLY ☐ HIS REPLY

☐ HIS REPLY ☐ HER REPLY

# How can you monitor the real world?

☐ HER REPLY ☐ HIS REPLY

☐ HIS REPLY ☐ HER REPLY

Do you want to say something to your father? What is it?

☐ HER REPLY  ☐ HIS REPLY                    ☐ HIS REPLY  ☐ HER REPLY

Can you teach your children what is good? How?

☐ HER REPLY  ☐ HIS REPLY                    ☐ HIS REPLY  ☐ HER REPLY

## So what kind of life are you moving back to?

☐ HER REPLY  ☐ HIS REPLY

☐ HIS REPLY  ☐ HER REPLY

## How would you describe the feeling of being so emotionally balanced?

☐ HER REPLY  ☐ HIS REPLY

☐ HIS REPLY  ☐ HER REPLY

# What are the things you do every single day?

☐ HER REPLY  ☐ HIS REPLY

☐ HIS REPLY  ☐ HER REPLY

# How can you respond to non-verbal communication when you are hearing them?

☐ HER REPLY  ☐ HIS REPLY

☐ HIS REPLY  ☐ HER REPLY

# What do your best friends say that you do right about yourself?

☐ HER REPLY ☐ HIS REPLY

☐ HIS REPLY ☐ HER REPLY

# How would you describe the feeling of being informed?

☐ HER REPLY ☐ HIS REPLY

☐ HIS REPLY ☐ HER REPLY

# If you could be happy, would you and why?

☐ HER REPLY ☐ HIS REPLY      ☐ HIS REPLY ☐ HER REPLY

# What was your favorite family dinner as a child?

☐ HER REPLY ☐ HIS REPLY      ☐ HIS REPLY ☐ HER REPLY

What would happen if you threw a piece of trash on the ground? What if everyone did?

☐ HER REPLY ☐ HIS REPLY

☐ HIS REPLY ☐ HER REPLY

What is the best thing to do in a situation in which someone gets mad?

☐ HER REPLY ☐ HIS REPLY

☐ HIS REPLY ☐ HER REPLY

# Describe the most ludicrous outfit you can think of

☐ HER REPLY ☐ HIS REPLY

☐ HIS REPLY ☐ HER REPLY

# If you had to choose one thing as the defining trait for a woman, what would it be?

☐ HER REPLY ☐ HIS REPLY

☐ HIS REPLY ☐ HER REPLY

# How would you describe the feeling of being just?

☐ HER REPLY ☐ HIS REPLY

☐ HIS REPLY ☐ HER REPLY

# What's the weirdest thing a guest has done at your house?

☐ HER REPLY ☐ HIS REPLY

☐ HIS REPLY ☐ HER REPLY

How would you describe the feeling of being closed away like there's someone inside you?

☐ HER REPLY ☐ HIS REPLY          ☐ HIS REPLY ☐ HER REPLY

What does it mean when someone asks you what it means to not be afraid of death?

☐ HER REPLY ☐ HIS REPLY          ☐ HIS REPLY ☐ HER REPLY

# Why would you rather use your body?

☐ HER REPLY  ☐ HIS REPLY

☐ HIS REPLY  ☐ HER REPLY

# How would you be different if you had never watched television?

☐ HER REPLY  ☐ HIS REPLY

☐ HIS REPLY  ☐ HER REPLY

If you could pick just one person to be your coach, who would it be and why?

☐ HER REPLY   ☐ HIS REPLY

☐ HIS REPLY   ☐ HER REPLY

Does the lifestyle you want for you and your loved ones align with what you think is right for you right now?

☐ HER REPLY   ☐ HIS REPLY

☐ HIS REPLY   ☐ HER REPLY

*If you could, would you go back in time and do something differently from what you were doing?*

☐ HER REPLY   ☐ HIS REPLY

☐ HIS REPLY   ☐ HER REPLY

*What lies do you most often tell yourself?*

☐ HER REPLY   ☐ HIS REPLY

☐ HIS REPLY   ☐ HER REPLY

# What is one thing that sets you apart from everyone else?

☐ HER REPLY  ☐ HIS REPLY

☐ HIS REPLY  ☐ HER REPLY

# What's your relationship with technology?

☐ HER REPLY  ☐ HIS REPLY

☐ HIS REPLY  ☐ HER REPLY

☐ HER REPLY  ☐ HIS REPLY          ☐ HIS REPLY  ☐ HER REPLY



☐ HER REPLY  ☐ HIS REPLY          ☐ HIS REPLY  ☐ HER REPLY

If you had to choose only one player to have with you to the
final game, who would it be?

☐ HER REPLY ☐ HIS REPLY          ☐ HIS REPLY ☐ HER REPLY

What is the most significant thing you have seen in your career
thus far?

☐ HER REPLY ☐ HIS REPLY          ☐ HIS REPLY ☐ HER REPLY

# What are you looking forward to seeing?

☐ HER REPLY ☐ HIS REPLY

☐ HIS REPLY ☐ HER REPLY

# What is the funniest name you have heard used in the real world?

☐ HER REPLY ☐ HIS REPLY

☐ HIS REPLY ☐ HER REPLY

*Would you rather wear a bathing suit or wear formal attire everywhere you go for the next two weeks? Why?*

☐ HER REPLY  ☐ HIS REPLY

☐ HIS REPLY  ☐ HER REPLY

## Which food do you prefer?

☐ HER REPLY  ☐ HIS REPLY

☐ HIS REPLY  ☐ HER REPLY

# How did you help your children learn social skills?

☐ HER REPLY ☐ HIS REPLY

___________________________

___________________________

___________________________

___________________________

___________________________

___________________________

___________________________

___________________________

___________________________

☐ HIS REPLY ☐ HER REPLY

___________________________

___________________________

___________________________

___________________________

___________________________

___________________________

___________________________

___________________________

___________________________

# What are your personal experiences as a mentor?

☐ HER REPLY ☐ HIS REPLY

___________________________

___________________________

___________________________

___________________________

___________________________

___________________________

___________________________

___________________________

☐ HIS REPLY ☐ HER REPLY

___________________________

___________________________

___________________________

___________________________

___________________________

___________________________

___________________________

___________________________

# Describe your family vacation

☐ HER REPLY  ☐ HIS REPLY

☐ HIS REPLY  ☐ HER REPLY

# What's something you always forget?

☐ HER REPLY  ☐ HIS REPLY

☐ HIS REPLY  ☐ HER REPLY

## If you could be any non-dinosaur animal, what would you be?

☐ HER REPLY  ☐ HIS REPLY

☐ HIS REPLY  ☐ HER REPLY

## What other aspects of your life would you like to focus on?

☐ HER REPLY  ☐ HIS REPLY

☐ HIS REPLY  ☐ HER REPLY

# What is the one thing you can't change about your body language?

☐ HER REPLY ☐ HIS REPLY

☐ HIS REPLY ☐ HER REPLY

---

# What is your point?

☐ HER REPLY ☐ HIS REPLY

☐ HIS REPLY ☐ HER REPLY

# Who were your inspirations?

☐ HER REPLY  ☐ HIS REPLY          ☐ HIS REPLY  ☐ HER REPLY

# Would you rather be alone for a few hours or longer?

☐ HER REPLY  ☐ HIS REPLY          ☐ HIS REPLY  ☐ HER REPLY

What was it like to be around thousands of people dressed up
like actors?

☐ HER REPLY  ☐ HIS REPLY                    ☐ HIS REPLY  ☐ HER REPLY

What is one thing you have in common with the person whom
you met a while ago?

☐ HER REPLY  ☐ HIS REPLY                    ☐ HIS REPLY  ☐ HER REPLY

If you could sum up a day for just one sentence in terms of what you saw and what you thought, what will you write about?

☐ HER REPLY  ☐ HIS REPLY

☐ HIS REPLY  ☐ HER REPLY

Tell about a memorable experience from your formal education.

☐ HER REPLY  ☐ HIS REPLY

☐ HIS REPLY  ☐ HER REPLY

## What is your perfect book title to describe your life so far?

☐ HER REPLY ☐ HIS REPLY

☐ HIS REPLY ☐ HER REPLY

## What do you believe is the most important thing in life?

☐ HER REPLY ☐ HIS REPLY

☐ HIS REPLY ☐ HER REPLY

*How would you describe the feeling of being suffocated?*

☐ HER REPLY   ☐ HIS REPLY

☐ HIS REPLY   ☐ HER REPLY

*What is the one thing that bugs you about fast food today?*

☐ HER REPLY   ☐ HIS REPLY

☐ HIS REPLY   ☐ HER REPLY

# What did you see that you liked a lot?

☐ HER REPLY  ☐ HIS REPLY

☐ HIS REPLY  ☐ HER REPLY

# What's been your most awkward experience?

☐ HER REPLY  ☐ HIS REPLY

☐ HIS REPLY  ☐ HER REPLY

## What is the most ludicrous outfit you can think of?

☐ HER REPLY ☐ HIS REPLY

☐ HIS REPLY ☐ HER REPLY

## Talk about the dream that you had last night.

☐ HER REPLY ☐ HIS REPLY

☐ HIS REPLY ☐ HER REPLY

# How would you feel if you were going to be on TV?

☐ HER REPLY  ☐ HIS REPLY

☐ HIS REPLY  ☐ HER REPLY

# If you could change your name to any other name, what would it be and why?

☐ HER REPLY  ☐ HIS REPLY

☐ HIS REPLY  ☐ HER REPLY

# Do you think that your purpose is to achieve more by achieving less?

☐ HER REPLY  ☐ HIS REPLY          ☐ HIS REPLY  ☐ HER REPLY

# What are your deciding factors?

☐ HER REPLY  ☐ HIS REPLY          ☐ HIS REPLY  ☐ HER REPLY

# Say something about your current mood.

☐ HER REPLY ☐ HIS REPLY      ☐ HIS REPLY ☐ HER REPLY

# What are three things you'd love to find out about?

☐ HER REPLY ☐ HIS REPLY      ☐ HIS REPLY ☐ HER REPLY

How would you describe the feeling of being the link between the realm of shadows and the world above?

☐ HER REPLY  ☐ HIS REPLY      ☐ HIS REPLY  ☐ HER REPLY

Would you rather have a non-human or a robot?

☐ HER REPLY  ☐ HIS REPLY      ☐ HIS REPLY  ☐ HER REPLY

What is one thing that you would like to see a change in our country that would make you very happy?

☐ HER REPLY  ☐ HIS REPLY          ☐ HIS REPLY  ☐ HER REPLY

With the hope of preserving family history, describe the kinds of questions to ask an older relative.

☐ HER REPLY  ☐ HIS REPLY          ☐ HIS REPLY  ☐ HER REPLY

# Say something about what has happened

☐ HER REPLY  ☐ HIS REPLY

☐ HIS REPLY  ☐ HER REPLY

# Do you ever feel lonely? Why?

☐ HER REPLY  ☐ HIS REPLY

☐ HIS REPLY  ☐ HER REPLY

# What's the funniest thing you saw this week?

☐ HER REPLY ☐ HIS REPLY          ☐ HIS REPLY ☐ HER REPLY

# What's the weirdest thing you've ever done?

☐ HER REPLY ☐ HIS REPLY          ☐ HIS REPLY ☐ HER REPLY

# Who is the person you look up to?

☐ HER REPLY ☐ HIS REPLY                    ☐ HIS REPLY ☐ HER REPLY

# Why is it that sometimes life seems unfair?

☐ HER REPLY ☐ HIS REPLY                    ☐ HIS REPLY ☐ HER REPLY

# How do you know when you're being watched?

☐ HER REPLY  ☐ HIS REPLY                    ☐ HIS REPLY  ☐ HER REPLY

# Tell about an experience you had while volunteering your help.

☐ HER REPLY  ☐ HIS REPLY                    ☐ HIS REPLY  ☐ HER REPLY

# What do you like to do when you're bored?

☐ HER REPLY  ☐ HIS REPLY

☐ HIS REPLY  ☐ HER REPLY

# What are your 3 most common mental habits that keep you from being happy?

☐ HER REPLY  ☐ HIS REPLY

☐ HIS REPLY  ☐ HER REPLY

# What was it about it that got you interested?

☐ HER REPLY  ☐ HIS REPLY

☐ HIS REPLY  ☐ HER REPLY

# What's the best part about it?

☐ HER REPLY  ☐ HIS REPLY

☐ HIS REPLY  ☐ HER REPLY

# What is important to you in life and why?

☐ HER REPLY  ☐ HIS REPLY                    ☐ HIS REPLY  ☐ HER REPLY

# Have you done anything that would help you get by without help?

☐ HER REPLY  ☐ HIS REPLY                    ☐ HIS REPLY  ☐ HER REPLY

# What's the worst thing about being a child?

☐ HER REPLY  ☐ HIS REPLY

☐ HIS REPLY  ☐ HER REPLY

# What is the big deal to you about what happened today?

☐ HER REPLY  ☐ HIS REPLY

☐ HIS REPLY  ☐ HER REPLY

## If there was only one superhero to fight for you, who would that be?

☐ HER REPLY  ☐ HIS REPLY

☐ HIS REPLY  ☐ HER REPLY

## What are the last thoughts you have when you wake up in the morning?

☐ HER REPLY  ☐ HIS REPLY

☐ HIS REPLY  ☐ HER REPLY

How would you describe the feeling of being in a band on the road?

☐ HER REPLY  ☐ HIS REPLY                    ☐ HIS REPLY  ☐ HER REPLY

If you had to choose between being able to fly and being able to swim, which would you choose? Why?

☐ HER REPLY  ☐ HIS REPLY                    ☐ HIS REPLY  ☐ HER REPLY

## What is one thing you have in common with your son?

☐ HER REPLY  ☐ HIS REPLY                    ☐ HIS REPLY  ☐ HER REPLY

## What changes would you be making that are important?

☐ HER REPLY  ☐ HIS REPLY                    ☐ HIS REPLY  ☐ HER REPLY

# List of things that have been done

☐ HER REPLY  ☐ HIS REPLY

☐ HIS REPLY  ☐ HER REPLY

# What is the one thing that you have that keeps you going?

☐ HER REPLY  ☐ HIS REPLY

☐ HIS REPLY  ☐ HER REPLY

What is the one thing you've come to regret the most in your
life in the last ten years?

☐ HER REPLY ☐ HIS REPLY          ☐ HIS REPLY ☐ HER REPLY

What would be something you would do to relax?

☐ HER REPLY ☐ HIS REPLY          ☐ HIS REPLY ☐ HER REPLY

# What makes you feel like you'll live forever?

☐ HER REPLY  ☐ HIS REPLY

☐ HIS REPLY  ☐ HER REPLY

# What song have you learned the most from?

☐ HER REPLY  ☐ HIS REPLY

☐ HIS REPLY  ☐ HER REPLY

## What is something you do that makes you feel so beautiful?

☐ HER REPLY  ☐ HIS REPLY

☐ HIS REPLY  ☐ HER REPLY

## When someone picks on someone else, how do you feel? What do you do?

☐ HER REPLY  ☐ HIS REPLY

☐ HIS REPLY  ☐ HER REPLY

## What does your child look for in a boyfriend/girlfriend?

☐ HER REPLY  ☐ HIS REPLY

☐ HIS REPLY  ☐ HER REPLY

## What is the difference between a normal day and a boring day?

☐ HER REPLY  ☐ HIS REPLY

☐ HIS REPLY  ☐ HER REPLY

# Say something about the smell of you

☐ HER REPLY  ☐ HIS REPLY          ☐ HIS REPLY  ☐ HER REPLY

# What is your true essence and identity?

☐ HER REPLY  ☐ HIS REPLY          ☐ HIS REPLY  ☐ HER REPLY

# What was it that you were most seeking and why?

☐ HER REPLY  ☐ HIS REPLY

☐ HIS REPLY  ☐ HER REPLY

# What would you say your top ten is?

☐ HER REPLY  ☐ HIS REPLY

☐ HIS REPLY  ☐ HER REPLY

If you were an animal, what would be your greatest desire at this point in your life?

☐ HER REPLY  ☐ HIS REPLY

☐ HIS REPLY  ☐ HER REPLY

What was the big picture before, during, and after that moment? Did you do anything about it or did you just sit there and do nothing?

☐ HER REPLY  ☐ HIS REPLY

☐ HIS REPLY  ☐ HER REPLY

# When was the first time you experienced it?

☐ HER REPLY ☐ HIS REPLY

_______________________________

☐ HIS REPLY ☐ HER REPLY

_______________________________

# At what age did you learn to ride a bicycle?

☐ HER REPLY ☐ HIS REPLY

_______________________________

☐ HIS REPLY ☐ HER REPLY

_______________________________

# Would you rather be able to command water or the wind? Why?

☐ HER REPLY  ☐ HIS REPLY

☐ HIS REPLY  ☐ HER REPLY

# Would you rather have a hot dog or fries that are greasy and full of fat?

☐ HER REPLY  ☐ HIS REPLY

☐ HIS REPLY  ☐ HER REPLY

# How do you make moves?

☐ HER REPLY  ☐ HIS REPLY

☐ HIS REPLY  ☐ HER REPLY

# Does it give you a new idea about what to expect?

☐ HER REPLY  ☐ HIS REPLY

☐ HIS REPLY  ☐ HER REPLY